CALIFORNIA

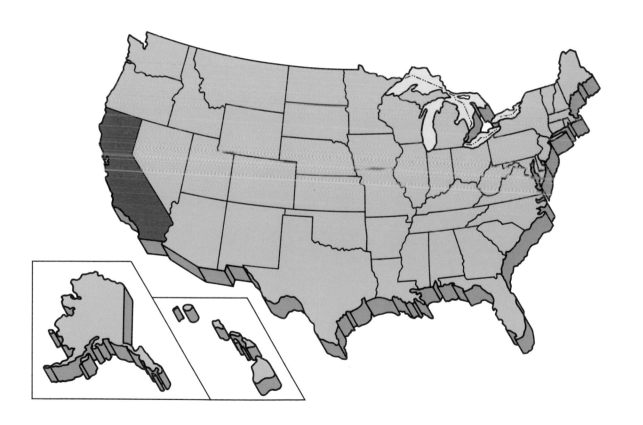

CALIFORNIA

Kathy Pelta

 Lerner Publications Company

LIBRARY OF CONGRESS
CATALOGING-IN-PUBLICATION DATA
Pelta, Kathy.
    California / by Kathy Pelta.
      p. cm. — (Hello USA)
    Includes index.
    Summary: Introduces the geography, history,
people, industries, and environmental concerns
of the Golden State.
    ISBN 0-8225-2738-3 (lib. bdg.)
    1. California—Juvenile literature. 2.
California—Geography—Juvenile literature.
[1. California.] I. Title. II. Series.
F861.3.P45 1994
979.4—dc20   93-1497
                                    CIP
                                     AC

Manufactured in the United States of America

1 2 3 4 5 6 - I/JR - 99 98 97 96 95 94

Cover photograph by Kent & Donna Dannen.

The glossary that begins on page 68 gives defini-
tions of words shown in **bold type** in the text.

 This book is printed on
acid-free, recyclable paper.

CONTENTS

Did You Know . . . ?

❏ The Golden Gate Bridge in San Francisco is one of the longest suspension bridges in the world. It spans 6,450 feet (1,966 meters) of water at the entrance to San Francisco Bay.

Giant sequoia

❏ The biggest and oldest trees in the world grow in California. Redwoods are the tallest, sweeping the sky at more than 300 feet (91 m). Giant sequoias have trunks that measure more than 25 feet (8 m) from side to side. And some bristlecone pines are more than 4,000 years old!

❏ Levi's denim jeans were first made in California in 1874. Levi Strauss made the pants tough enough to withstand hard wear by miners. He used heavy canvas with brass rivets to reinforce the seams. The design has been popular ever since.

❏ You can experience the shakes of an earthquake by entering artificial "safequakes" at Universal Studios in Los Angeles and at the planetarium in San Francisco.

❏ Every year on March 19, people from all over the world come to San Juan Capistrano, California, to watch thousands of swallows return from their winter homes.

❏ About 40,000 years ago, prehistoric animals became trapped in a gooey mess at the La Brea Tar Pits in Los Angeles. The animals got stuck in the murky tar that lay under a pool of water. Scientists are still digging out the remains.

A Trip Around the State

Golden poppies carpet California's meadows in spring. Each summer, grassy hills turn golden brown. Golden sunshine beams year-round. No wonder California is called the Golden State. The Golden State also has jagged mountains, sun-baked deserts, cool redwood forests, and miles and miles of sandy beaches.

The beaches line the Pacific Ocean, which borders California on the west. The state's coast stretches from Oregon in the north all the way to Mexico in the south, a distance of about 900 miles (1,448 kilometers). California's neighbors to the east are Arizona, which lies across the Colorado River, and Nevada.

The golden poppy *(above)* **is California's state flower. Other golden flowers** *(facing page)* **dot the coast in spring, while the sun scorches desert areas** *(inset).*

Lava formations jut up on Lassen Peak, an active volcano in the Cascade Mountains.

California can be divided into four geographic regions. They are the Coast Ranges, the Inland Mountains, the Central Valley, and the Great Basin. The Coast Ranges stretch the entire length of California along the Pacific Ocean. Most of the mountains in these ranges are low, but some peaks of the Klamath Mountains in the north reach up to 8,000 feet (2,438 m).

The Inland Mountains also run lengthwise. Their two major ranges—the Cascade Mountains and the Sierra Nevada—contain some of the highest peaks in the United States, including Mount Whitney at 14,494 feet (4,418 m). Volcanoes created the Cascades millions of years ago, when fiery melted rock called lava oozed out of the earth's crust and hardened into mountains.

Long ago, **glaciers,** or slowly moving rivers of ice, covered the high parts of the Sierra Nevada and carved deep canyons. Later the glaciers melted, creating hundreds of streams and lakes, including Lake Tahoe.

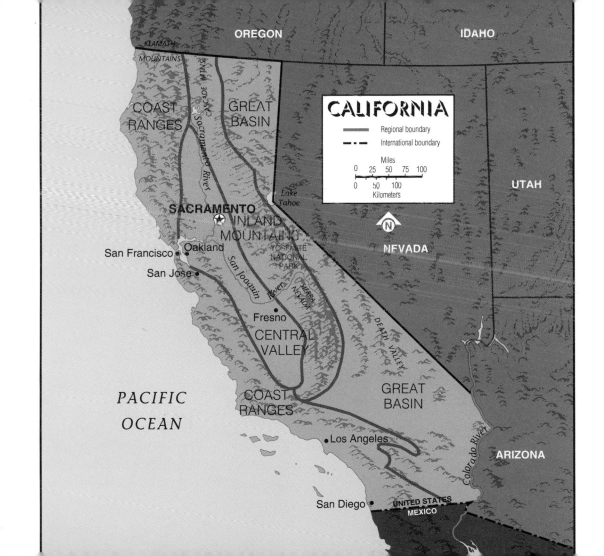

From Yosemite Valley in the Sierra Nevada rise the sheer rock walls of Half Dome *(left)*. East of the valley, high in the Sierra, calcium deposits transform Mono Lake *(above)* into a moonlike landscape.

Lush farmland stretches across California's Central Valley.

The long, flat Central Valley separates the Coast Ranges from the Inland Mountains. Fertile soil has made the Central Valley California's best farmland. Two of the state's major rivers—the Sacramento and the San Joaquin—flow through the region. These waterways join near the capital city of Sacramento and together flow west into San Francisco Bay. From there, a **strait** (water passageway) called the Golden Gate leads to the Pacific Ocean.

13

Deserts in California range from cracked mud to sand dunes to rocky mountains.

In the Great Basin, California's driest region, soil cracks from lack of rain. A method of watering land called **irrigation** allows farmers to work dry land in some areas. But in most of the region, vast deserts stretch for miles. One area of the Great Basin is so hot and dry it was named Death Valley to warn travelers to stay away.

Death Valley once recorded a scorching temperature of 134° F (57° C). Summer highs of 120° F (49° C) are normal for California's inland valleys, but winters bring freezing temperatures. Along the northern coast, people shiver during cool, foggy summers and rainy, cold winters but autumns are warm and sunny. Southern Californians enjoy mild weather, sea breezes, and sunshine most of the year.

No matter where people live in the state, they can divide the year into two seasons—one dry and one wet. From May to October, it rarely rains anywhere. In the winter, rain falls mostly in the north and snow covers the mountains. Annual rainfall varies from 2 inches (5 centimeters) in desert areas to 100 inches (254 cm) along the northern coast.

Who Gets the Water?

Californians depend on the rain and snow that fall during the wet season to provide them with water all year long. To store water, the state has built reservoirs, or artificial lakes. Falling rain and melting snow fill mountain streams that flow into the reservoirs. Then aqueducts, or canals, carry the water to all parts of the state.

When rainfall is lower than usual, the reservoirs can't provide enough water to go around, and everyone must help to conserve it. By law, more than half of California's water goes to farmers. Yet urban areas, especially in the south, keep growing and needing more water. This leads to one of the state's biggest problems—who gets the water? The question has no easy answers, and the debate continues.

Low rainfall can be a serious threat. Another one is earthquakes. Most earthquakes are small and cause no damage, but major quakes can topple buildings, bridges, and freeways in a few seconds. Earthquakes occur along **fault lines**, where sections of the earth's crust meet and rub against each other,

In 1906 San Francisco suffered a devastating earthquake *(left)*. Although it lasted only 90 seconds, the tremor set off fires that raged for three days.

causing the earth to shake. The longest fault in the state, the San Andreas Fault, extends from northern California to Mexico.

Like landforms and climates in California, a wide variety of animals and plants exist in the state. Rattlesnakes, lizards, and tortoises rest in the shade of desert cactuses, while bighorn sheep climb among bristlecone pines in the high country.

Bristlecone pines are named for their prickly pinecones.

The condor, which is nearly extinct, is the largest flying bird in North America. With a wingspan of more than eight feet (2.4 m), it soars over scrub oaks in the foothills of southern California, while peregrine falcons nest in the rocky cliffs of Yosemite National Park in the Sierra Nevada.

California's state animal, the grizzly bear, no longer inhabits the Golden State, but black bears still roam in the mountains. Cougars and mountain lions prey on the many deer that thrive throughout the state. On rocky coasts, sea lions play. On sandy beaches, elephant seals bask in the sun. Whales swim offshore, and occasionally pass through the Golden Gate into San Francisco Bay!

A mountain lion *(above)* rests in the shade, while elephant seals *(right)* relax on the beach. A peregrine falcon *(far right)* perches on a rocky cliff.

19

California's Story

Chumash artists
painted symbols on
rocks in caves.

About 12,000 years ago, the first people to come
to what is now California arrived from the north
and the east. Over many centuries, groups struggled across the rugged mountains and vast
deserts that now form California's borders.
Descendants of these people are called American Indians, or Native Americans.

Somewhere between 200 and 500 different Indian nations, or tribes, eventually settled in
what is now California. Each nation spoke its
own language and had its own way of life.

The nations of the southern coast were among
the largest. Some villages built by the Chumash
Indians had more than 1,000 people. Skilled
fishermen from several nations traveled the sea
in oceangoing canoes, gathering shellfish and
other sea creatures for food.

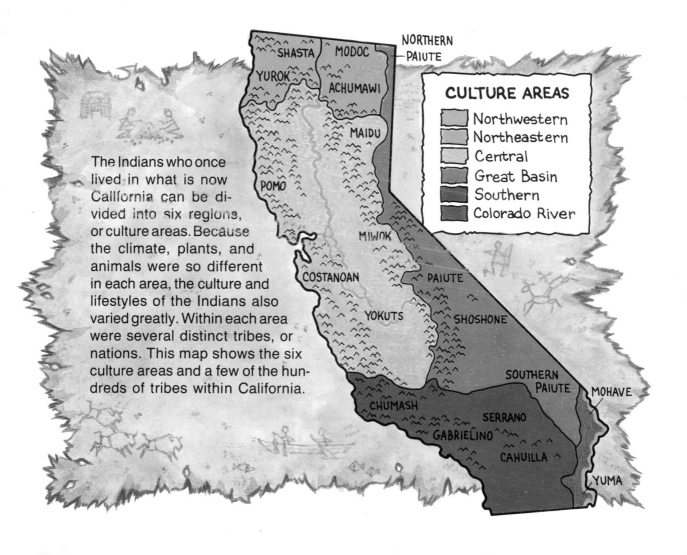

The Indians who once lived in what is now California can be divided into six regions, or culture areas. Because the climate, plants, and animals were so different in each area, the culture and lifestyles of the Indians also varied greatly. Within each area were several distinct tribes, or nations. This map shows the six culture areas and a few of the hundreds of tribes within California.

NORTHERN PAIUTE

CULTURE AREAS

- Northwestern
- Northeastern
- Central
- Great Basin
- Southern
- Colorado River

SHASTA
MODOC
YUROK
ACHUMAWI
MAIDU
POMO
MIWOK
COSTANOAN
PAIUTE
YOKUTS
SHOSHONE
SOUTHERN PAIUTE
MOHAVE
CHUMASH
SERRANO
GABRIELINO
CAHUILLA
YUMA

Indian homes varied from one location to another. In Yosemite Valley *(left)*, the Miwok gathered thick slabs of bark from forests to construct their lodges. In the Sacramento Valley *(right)*, the Maidu covered their lodges with cool earth to keep out the hot sun.

To the north, abundant plant and animal life provided plenty of food. In what is now central California, the most important food source was the acorn, which comes from oak trees. Using stones, the women pounded dried acorns into powder to make cakes or a boiled cereal like oatmeal.

Central nations each had several villages scattered far apart, giving villagers enough space to hunt and gather food. Trespassing was usually forbidden, so members of a nation had little contact with neighboring communities. Each village had a leader to give advice, and men and women called shamans performed religious ceremonies. In ceremonies to cure illness, the shaman danced or sang, blew smoke on the part that hurt, or tried to suck out the source of pain.

In the Klamath Mountains to the north, the Indians shared some customs with those of central peoples. Food, clothing, and the use of shamans were similar. But northern nations valued possessions more than their southern neighbors did. The richest men—those who had the most woodpecker scalps, white deerskins, and seashells—were the leaders.

Along the eastern strip of what is now California, dry weather made food and water scarce. The Indians in this area had to spend most of their time searching for food. Life along the Colorado River in the southeast was a little easier. Here, the Indians channeled water from the river to grow crops such as corn, beans, and pumpkins. The southeastern nations were the most organized in all of the region. They united to fight wars, and they traveled far to trade with other nations.

Indians in what is now California probably never saw a white person until the mid-1500s. At that time, Spaniards in search of gold found what they thought was an island near the west coast of

Mapmakers in the 1500s and 1600s drew California as an island.

Mexico. They called the island California, after a treasure island they had read about in a book.

But this part of California, called Baja (Lower) California, turned out to be a **peninsula**, not an island. And it had no treasure. So the king of Spain sent Juan Rodríguez Cabrillo north to explore the region beyond Baja California. In 1542 Cabrillo sailed into San Diego Bay, becoming the first European to visit Alta (Upper) California. Finding no gold, he soon left.

The next European visitor, England's Sir Francis Drake, did not stay long either. His ship stopped north of what is now San Francisco in 1579, and he claimed the land for his country's queen. Drake then sailed home, never to return.

Francis Drake greeted coastal Indians on his brief stop near San Francisco Bay.

Russian fur traders who had built an outpost in northern California soon left, too. For nearly another 200 years, the Indians in California lived undisturbed by outsiders. Mountains, deserts, and the ocean isolated them from other people.

25

In 1769 Spain acted to secure its claim to this land. Spanish soldiers built a presidio, or fort, in what is now San Diego, and Father Junípero Serra and some other Catholic priests from Spain set up a **mission**. By the early 1820s, 4 presidios and 21 missions dotted the California coast.

The missions were part church

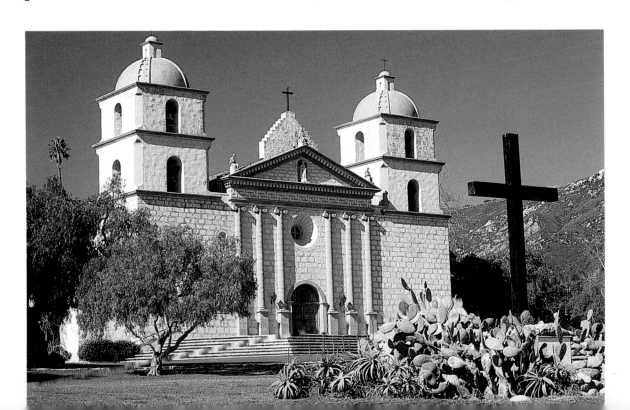

Some missions, such as Santa Barbara *(facing page),* **eventually expanded into thriving cities. At the presidios** *(right),* **Spanish guards treated Indian workers like slaves.**

and part pueblo, or town. Father Serra's plan was to teach coastal Indians the Catholic religion. He also taught them how to make adobe (clay) bricks and how to irrigate fields, tend crops, and raise cattle.

At the missions, the Indians were forced to work and to worship. They had to give up their old ways of life, their own foods, and their traditional religions. Many tried to run away, only to be captured and flogged or put in chains as a warning to others.

Within a few years, thousands of mission Indians died from European diseases such as measles and smallpox. When the Spaniards first arrived, 300,000 Indians lived in California. Fewer than 150,000 remained in 1821, when Mexico—which included California—won its independence from Spain.

As an independent nation, Mexico ended the mission system. Much of the missionary land was divided into large estates called ranchos. Although Spanish officials had promised land to the Indians, it now was given mainly to Mexican settlers. With no property of their own, many Indians were stuck working on the ranchos for little or no money.

Unlike Spain, Mexico allowed outsiders to come to its territories. Trading ships from the East Coast of the United States docked at California's ports to load cowhides and animal furs. U.S. trappers blazed mountain trails to the West Coast, and pioneers soon followed in covered wagons. Still, by 1845 the population of California, not including Indians, was only 7,000.

In 1846 U.S. Army captain John C. Frémont arrived in California. When a band of Americans made plans for California to break away from Mexico, Frémont helped them. On June 14, 1846, the men stormed Sonoma presidio and hoisted a homemade flag painted with a grizzly bear and the words "California Republic."

The Bear Flag republic lasted only three weeks. By then the United States and Mexico were at war over a border dispute. Most of the fighting took place in Texas. In California, Mexican soldiers surrendered after a few skirmishes. When the Mexican War ended California became a U.S. territory.

Disaster at Donner Pass

During the 1840s, pioneers began moving west to California. The journey was long and difficult. Stretches of desert and steep, rocky mountains were especially hard to cross.

In 1846 a group of families from Illinois organized by George Donner loaded their wagons and headed west. By the time the Donner party reached Wyoming, they were already behind schedule. When they heard of a shortcut across Utah, they decided to try their luck.

Unfortunately, the person who had recommended the new route had never actually taken it. The Donner party discovered that the shortcut actually took longer because it was so treacherous. By the time the group reached the top of the Sierra Nevada in early November, a snowstorm made it impossible to cross the mountains.

The Donner party realized they would have to settle in for the winter. They quickly made makeshift cabins. As food ran short, the pioneers struggled to find anything to eat—twigs, mice, their dogs, shoes. People grew weak and sick. Some died.

By mid-December they decided to send 17 people ahead to try and get help. Half died of cold and starvation, and it was more than a month before one member reached a town. Rescue teams with food set out in February.

Meanwhile, food grew even scarcer in the mountain camp. As cold and hunger made the survivors more and more desperate, they began carving up and cooking the people who had died.

By the time the last rescue team finally arrived, almost half of the 87 members of the Donner party had died. In memory of the tragedy, the path they took over the mountains is named Donner Pass.

California's state flag is patterned after the flag raised during the Bear Flag revolt. The lone star represented California as an independent republic. The grizzly bear was meant to warn the Mexican army that the Californian rebels were willing to fight for freedom from Mexico.

The peace **treaty** that ended the Mexican War was signed on February 2, 1848. Only days before, an amazing discovery had been made at Sutter's sawmill in the foothills east of Sacramento. James Marshall, an American working at the mill, saw something shining in a stream. It was gold!

Mill workers tried to keep the discovery secret. But word quickly leaked out—the gold rush was on. Adventurers from all over the world headed for California. By

1849, 40,000 gold seekers—nicknamed forty-niners after the year in which they came—were swarming over the gold-rich country. That year they took out $30 million worth of nuggets and gold dust.

African Americans and the Gold Rush

Among the many newcomers to California during the gold rush were African Americans. Some were slaves who came from Southern states to work in the mines and use their earnings to buy their freedom. Moses Rodgers, for example, worked his way out of slavery and gained fame as one of the best mining engineers in California. Many black miners saved money to free relatives still held as slaves in the South.

Some black newcomers became rich by providing services to the gold diggers. Some set up shops. Mifflin Gibbs was one of the owners of the only shoe store in San Francisco during the gold rush. George Dennis rented a gambling table at the Eldorado Hotel in San Francisco. His mother used the table to sell hot meals to gamblers at huge profits.

With many goods in short supply, prices were sky high. Shopkeepers could sell an apple or an egg for $1. A loaf of bread was 10 times the usual price, and medicine was $10 a pill. Some African Americans bought land cheaply and made a fortune selling it at much higher prices a few years later.

With wealth so easy to come by, a person's history or skin color didn't matter. San Francisco, a gateway to the gold country, became the state's largest city, bustling with bankers, traders, and merchants of all colors.

While the forty-niners were digging for gold, a group of lawmakers met in Monterey to write a constitution, or set of laws, for California. The constitution forbade slavery, but it also denied blacks, Native Americans, and women the right to vote. California's white males—the only people who could vote—approved the constitution in 1849. And on September 9, 1850, California became the 31st state in the Union.

By 1860 California's population had swelled to 300,000. But the number of Indians had dwindled to barely 30,000. Most had died from diseases brought by newcomers.

Although gold made California seem to many Americans like the land of their dreams, getting there wasn't easy. By ship, a journey from the country's East Coast could last three or four months. From the Midwest, a trip to California on the speediest overland stagecoach took 20 days.

To make travel easier, four Californians decided to build a railroad to hook up with tracks being laid from the East Coast. In 1861 these businessmen—Leland Stanford, Mark Hopkins, Charles Crocker, and Collis P. Huntington, known as the Big Four—formed the Central Pacific Company.

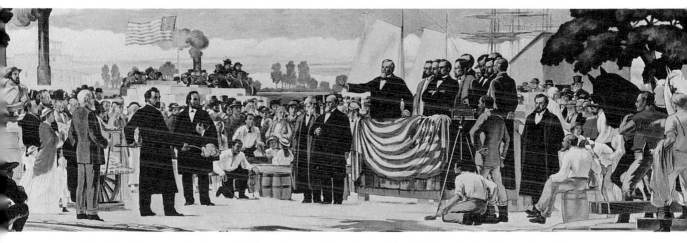

The Big Four and other Californians gather to celebrate the start of construction on the Central Pacific railroad. With the wealth they earned from the railway, the four men were able to bribe, or pay, lawmakers to vote for laws that helped the railroad business.

To solve the problem of finding workers, the Big Four brought 10,000 laborers from China to lay the tracks. In 1869 the eastern and western branches of the railroad met in Utah. With a silver hammer, officials drove in the final spike—made of California gold.

Chinese workers built railroad tracks across California.

It now took only seven days to make the journey from New York to California. No longer would

Railways opened the way for the state's farm goods to reach eastern markets, and passenger trains brought people west.

deserts and mountains isolate the state from the rest of the nation.

After the railroad was finished, Chinese workers competed with Americans for other jobs. The Chinese were willing to work for very low pay. White workers protested, crying, "California for Americans!" In 1882 the U.S. Congress passed a law to stop Chinese **immigrants** from coming.

Meanwhile, California businesspeople were urging vacationers to come to the Golden State to improve their health in the sunny climate of southern California. Railroads lured people west with cheap train tickets, and landholders in Los Angeles grew rich selling land to the new arrivals.

35

The glamour of the movie industry brought many people to the Golden State.

In the early 1900s, California attracted moviemakers, too. Besides sunny skies all year, southern California had a variety of background scenery—from deserts and cattle ranches to mountains and the seashore. Hollywood, a district in Los Angeles, soon became the motion-picture capital of the world.

Many people attracted by the movie industry found jobs in other new and growing industries. This was especially true during the 1920s, when a different type of gold—black gold, or oil—was discovered at three different sites near Los Angeles.

By this time, many Americans owned cars and needed gasoline (which is made from oil) to fuel their vehicles. Oil soon became Los Angeles's most important industry. Within a few years, the city passed San Francisco as California's largest urban area.

Since Los Angeles lay in a desert, the city was forced to pipe in water from the north. But with thousands of new people arriving each year, the city did not have enough water for everyone. In 1928 workers began building a dam across the Colorado River to collect more water. The dam permanently flooded land in the area, and hundreds of farmers and other people lost their property.

The Great Depression, a major slump in the nation's economy, struck in 1929. Businesses failed. Tourists no longer came to California to spend their dollars. Instead, jobless people flowed into the state, spurred by rumors of jobs. Many of the people were migrant workers, who moved from place to place to find jobs picking fruit and vegetables.

Having just sold the tires off the family's car to buy food, a migrant worker worries about where the next meal will come from.

California's businesses finally began to boom in 1941, when the United States entered World War II. Thousands of Americans in California's shipyards and defense plants built ships and planes for the war. Navy vessels swarmed in the harbors. Soldiers trained at camps around the state.

While California geared up for war, some people worried that the Japanese Americans living in the state might be spies for the enemy countries, which included Japan. In 1942 the U.S. government forced 93,000 Japanese Americans in California to leave their homes and move to inland camps. The prisoners were not allowed to leave the camps until late 1944.

During and after the war, people again moved west to California. Many soldiers who had been stationed in California brought their families to settle there. Thousands of African Americans moved to California to take jobs in factories. And new laws allowed more Asian and **Latino** immigrants into California.

Firefighters battle flames during the Watts riots of 1965.

Of all the different groups in California, African Americans became the most active in a movement for equality. They wanted the same chances for good housing, jobs, and schools that white Californians had.

Tension increased between white and black neighborhoods. In 1965 riots broke out in Watts, a black district in Los Angeles. Nearly 30 years later, in 1992, riots again broke out in Los Angeles when a California jury found four white policemen not guilty in the beating of a black motorist in the city.

10,000 B.C.	A.D.1542	1769	1849	1850	1882	1906

Native Americans first arrive in what is now California

Juan Rodriguez Cabrillo is the first European to visit California

Junípero Serra builds California's first mission at San Diego

California gold rush

California becomes the 31st state

Chinese immigration to the United States is stopped

San Francisco earthquake

With about 30 million people, California has other problems, too. Schools in many urban areas are overcrowded, and more and more cars clog the freeways and pollute the air.

Newcomers continue to flood into the state. At the same time, some Californians have chosen to leave for states with better job opportunities. For some, the Golden State may have lost its glitter, but for others it's a chance at a new beginning. Those who remain in the state are working to build a better future for all Californians.

1929	1942	1965	1992

Migrant workers begin flooding into California during the Great Depression

Japanese Americans in California are moved to prison camps during World War II

U.S. Immigration Act permits more people from Asia and Latin America to move to California

Los Angeles riots

Elementary-school students wave flags beside the woman they voted their favorite teacher. To be successful, California's teachers must be able to reach students from many different backgrounds.

Hordes of people admire sandcastles at a beach in San Diego.

Living and Working in California

Eureka! California's state motto is a Greek word that means "I've found it." In 1849 the forty-niners found gold. The pioneers who followed them west found hope and a chance to start a new life. Since California joined the Union in 1850, so many people have flocked to the state that it now has 30 million residents—more people than any other state in the country.

More and more immigrants—mainly from Mexico, Central and South America, and Southeast Asia—are looking for a new beginning in the Golden State. In fact, one out of every five people living in California was born in another country.

San Francisco's Chinatown bustles with activity.

43

With the nation's largest population, California is home to people from many places.

One in four Californians has Latin American roots. Some of these Latinos are descended from the Mexicans who lived in California when it was still part of Mexico. The three million people from Asia and the Pacific Islands represent about one-tenth of California's population. About two million African Americans live in the state.

Few of California's original American Indian nations have survived.

44

Most of the Indians living in California came from other states. The population numbers 242,000—fewer than 1 percent of all Californians. Some Indians live on **reservations**, or homelands set aside for them by the U.S. government.

Only 9 percent of Californians live in rural areas. The rest live in cities and suburbs, mostly near the coast. In the south are California's two largest cities—Los Angeles with 3.5 million people and San Diego with more than 1 million. Clustered in the San Francisco Bay area, the main cities in the north are San Jose, San Francisco, and Oakland. The fastest growing communities in the Central Valley are Fresno and Sacramento, the state capital.

One block of Lombard Street in San Francisco has so many turns that it's called the "crookedest street in the world."

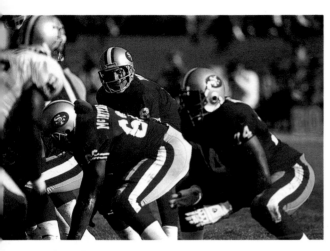

San Francisco 49ers

film capital of the world. Over the years, radio, television, and music recording have also become big businesses in California, entertaining millions of people worldwide.

California is a sports lover's dream. Professional teams include the Los Angeles Lakers and the Golden State Warriors for basketball, and the Oakland Athletics and the Los Angeles Dodgers for baseball. In football, the Los Angeles Rams, the Los Angeles Raiders, the San Diego Chargers, and the San Francisco 49ers all battle for their shot at the Super Bowl.

For recreation, many Californians head outdoors. At lakes and ocean beaches, people fish, surf,

Cities both north and south have art galleries, museums, theater groups, and symphony orchestras. San Francisco also boasts well-known opera and ballet companies.

Since the first movies were made in Hollywood in the early 1900s, southern California has been the

While most movies are made in Hollywood, some companies such as Paramount Pictures are based in the north.

sail, water-ski, or scuba dive. Campers can hike in one of California's many national, state, and county parks. In the winter, skiers swoosh down the snowy slopes of the Sierra Nevada and the Cascades.

Horseback riders enjoy the hills around Palm Springs.

Nearly every weekend a California city or town features a special event. Native Americans take part in games and traditional dances at powwows and fairs. Latino communities celebrate Mexican independence with fiestas on *Cinco de Mayo,* which means May 5 in Spanish. Parades with dragons and floats mark the Chinese New Year in San Francisco's Chinatown. In San Jose the Hoi Tet Festival celebrates the Vietnamese New Year.

Farming communities host festivals to honor crops from artichokes to zucchini. Pismo Beach has a clam-digging competition. And at the Gilroy Garlic Festival, people can even sample garlic ice cream!

Special events in California range from Mexican fiestas *(upper left)* **to festivals honoring asparagus** *(above)* **and garlic** *(lower left).*

49

Agriculture is a major industry in California, but only 3 percent of the state's workforce have jobs on farms. California grows more than half of the nation's fruits, vegetables, and nuts. Among the leading farm products are cotton, hay, wheat, poultry, and cattle. More grapes are

California's bountiful harvests include flowers *(left)* **and grapes** *(above).*

Each year, millions of tourists enter Fantasy Castle at Disneyland.

harvested in California than in any other state. They are sold as fresh fruit, dried to make raisins, or crushed to make wine and juice.

Many workers in California hold service jobs—that is, they help people or businesses. Three out of four Californians work in services, which includes government jobs and the booming tourist industry.

Many service workers have jobs in hotels, restaurants, resorts, and amusement parks such as Disneyland in Anaheim. Others drive buses, sell goods in stores, or work for banks, hospitals, or shipping companies.

Some of California's government jobs are with the Forest Service, which helps manage the state's parks and forests. Wildfires that burn forests and brush and threaten homes are a serious concern to Californians during the dry season.

California's first gold rush made the state wealthy, and workers still mine more gold than in any other state except Nevada. But nowadays oil earns the state much more money than gold does.

California's fishing industry operates out of harbors along the coast. Fishing crews catch shrimp, red snapper, tuna, and other fish

Much of California's logging industry is centered in northern towns such as Scotia.

Fishing crews mend their nets.

to sell throughout the country. Very few Californians—fewer than 1 percent—work in fishing or in mining.

Loggers cut down trees from northern California's forests for the state's wood-products industry. Although lumber sales are lower than previous years, California still provides more than 10 percent of the nation's lumber.

Factories employ 18 percent of the state's workforce, or 3 out of every 20 workers. These men and women may be engineers, machine operators, or technicians. Many of them design and assemble aircraft, space vehicles, and communication systems at aerospace centers in southern California.

53

Workers wear special suits *(above)* **so they won't contaminate the silicon used to make computer chips. In San Diego** *(right),* **boats sail in and out of the harbor.**

Some factories make electronic equipment and computers. Using a substance called silicon, workers build most of California's computer parts in a small area between San Jose and San Francisco—a region known as Silicon Valley.

With its varied goods and services, California has a state economy that is larger than the economies of many countries. Farms and businesses in California provide agricultural products and manufactured goods to other states and to the rest of the world.

The unspoiled wilderness around Lake Tahoe draws visitors throughout the year.

Protecting the Environment

California seems like a paradise to many people. It has mountain wilderness, peaceful beaches, and a long dry season that allows for all kinds of outdoor activities. But many Californians are concerned about a problem that threatens to spoil their paradise—air pollution.

California measures the highest levels of air pollution in the country. Most of the pollution is caused by burning **fossil fuels**—coal, oil, or natural gas—to produce energy.

Cars cause a lot of the pollution in California. Automobile engines get energy by burning gasoline, an oil product. This in turn produces car exhaust. The exhaust is made up of many gases, including carbon monoxide, nitrogen oxides, and unburned fuel.

When the unburned fuel and some other gases in car exhaust combine with sunlight, the mixture causes a hazy form of air pollution called **smog**. The word "smog" is a combination of the words "smoke" and "fog."

The mountains that border Los Angeles trap smog in the city.

By blocking the sun, smog creates hazy conditions in the Golden State and slows the growth of crops and other plants. Smog also makes eyes sting and can cause serious breathing problems.

Steady streams of traffic pollute the air.

Southern California's mountain ranges and climate worsen smoggy conditions. The mountains around Los Angeles trap gases in the city. Warm air and gases also become trapped in the area when weather conditions prevent the free flow of air.

One way to reduce air pollution is to make and drive vehicles designed to use fuel more efficiently. California's transportation companies are beginning to use vehicles that run on natural gas, methanol, or electricity. Experts hope that these fuels will not add as much to the smog problem.

California requires that all vehicles driven in crowded areas be tested regularly. The tests measure the levels of smog-forming gases in the exhaust from tailpipes. In fact, California started the strictest standards in the nation for this type of testing, called emissions testing.

The state also limits what people can burn. For example, some communities restrict the use of wood fires to reduce smoke in the air.

In some states, power plants are a big source of air pollution. Like many other states, California gets most of its electricity by burning fossil fuels. Some states burn coal. California, however, uses primarily natural gas. Natural gas is a much cleaner fuel to burn than coal is.

California also generates about one-fifth of its electricity from waterpower, which does not pollute the air at all. Dams built across streams high in the mountains trap melting snow. The power of the water is then used to turn big engines that produce electricity. The dams also provide water for farms and households. Dams do have some drawbacks, though. They can be especially hard on local wildlife populations.

Power companies in California use some other energy sources—such as windmills and nuclear power—that do not burn fossil fuels. Scientists are also developing ways to capture the energy from sunlight for use in solar power.

California is a leader in using sources of power that don't rely on fossil fuels. Windmills *(above)* supply electricity to some buildings, and, in Santa Cruz, even police officers *(right)* travel by bicycle.

Buying the equipment for these new technologies is expensive, and change is slow. The use of nuclear power has also been limited because waste materials and accidents at nuclear plants can be extremely dangerous to human health if they are not handled properly.

Everyone can help with some of the solutions to air pollution. For example, every time Californians choose to walk or ride a bike instead of driving, they are cutting down on the amount of car exhaust in the air. Sharing rides or taking the bus or the train also reduces the number of cars on the road. Through these and other efforts, Californians are doing their part to cut air pollution in the Golden State.

California's Famous People ━━━

Ansel Adams (1902–1984), from San Francisco, was a photographer of western landscapes. He became famous for his pictures of mountains, forests, and other wilderness areas. Adams also worked to preserve the nation's wilderness.

Martha Graham (1894–1991) was raised in Santa Barbara, California. At the age of 22, she began training in classical ballet. Graham soon developed her own style and started her own school and dance company, helping shape modern dance in the 1900s.

Julia Morgan (1872–1957), an architect from San Francisco, helped rebuild the city after the 1906 earthquake. During her career, Morgan designed more than 700 buildings, including the Hearst Castle at San Simeon, California.

▲ MARTHA GRAHAM

JULIA ▶
MORGAN

◀ STEVEN
JOBS

STEVEN ▶
WOZNIAK

INNOVATORS ━━━━━━━━━━

Ernest Gallo (born 1910) and **Julio Gallo** (1911–1993) were born in Modesto, California. The two brothers started making wine in 1933. Together, they built E & J Gallo into one of the nation's leading wineries.

Steven Jobs (born 1955) and **Steven Wozniak** (born 1950) met in Los Altos, California, at a summer job at Hewlett-Packard. The two went on to start Apple Computer in their garage in 1975. The business quickly grew to be one of the largest computer companies in the country.

MOVIE STARS

Shirley Temple Black (born 1928), a curly-haired child superstar of the 1930s, had roles in many movies, including *Heidi* and *The Little Princess*. Born in Santa Monica, Black went on to serve as U.S. ambassador to Ghana and to Czechoslovakia.

Clint Eastwood (born 1930) has starred in numerous movies, including *Dirty Harry*. Originally from San Francisco, Eastwood won an Oscar in 1993 as best director for *Unforgiven*.

Tom Hanks (born 1956) is a comedic actor from Concord, California. His box-office hits include *Splash*, *Sleepless in Seattle*, and *Big*, for which he won an Oscar as best actor in 1988.

Marilyn Monroe (1926–1962) was born in Los Angeles. Famous worldwide for her beauty, Monroe starred in several movies, including *Bus Stop*, *The Seven Year Itch*, and *Some Like It Hot*.

◄ TOM HANKS

▲ MARILYN MONROE

SHIRLEY
◄ TEMPLE
BLACK

◄ JERRY GARCIA

▼ MERLE HAGGARD

◄ NATALIE COLE

MUSICIANS

Natalie Cole (born 1950) is a rhythm-and-blues singer from Los Angeles. The daughter of Nat "King" Cole, Natalie Cole has won several awards, including two Grammy awards for her first album, *Inseparable*.

Jerry Garcia (born 1942), from San Francisco, is the founder, lead guitarist, and vocalist of the Grateful Dead. Formed in the 1960s and still popular, the band combines the sounds of bluegrass and folk music.

Merle Haggard (born 1937) was born in an abandoned refrigerator car in Bakersfield, California. His first career, as a petty thief, landed him in prison. Afterward, Haggard began singing country songs. His hits include "Mama Tried" and "Okie from Muskogee."

POLITICAL LEADERS

Thomas Bradley (born 1917) became the first black mayor of Los Angeles in 1973. Widely supported by both African Americans and whites, he was elected to five terms in a row. In 1984 Bradley won the Spingarn Medal for his work as a lawyer and for his leadership skills.

S. I. Hayakawa (1906–1992) was a Republican senator from California and the first Japanese American elected to the U.S. Senate. A college professor, Hayakawa also taught English at San Francisco State University and served as the school's president for four years.

Richard Nixon (born 1913), a native of Yorba Linda, California, was the 37th president of the United States. Noted for his skill in foreign affairs, Nixon reestablished U.S. relations with China. In 1974 he became the first president to resign from office due to his role in the Watergate Scandal (a break-in at the National Democratic Headquarters).

◀ THOMAS
BRADLEY

▲ S. I.
HAYAKAWA

◀ RICHARD
NIXON

JOE
DIMAGGIO ▶

SPORTS FIGURES

Joe DiMaggio (born 1914), from Martinez, California, is one of the greatest outfielders in baseball history. He also set a major-league record for the longest hitting streak, which lasted for 56 games in a row. DiMaggio, who played for the New York Yankees, was elected to the National Baseball Hall of Fame in 1955.

Florence Griffith Joyner (born 1959) started running at the age of seven in her hometown, Los Angeles. At the 1988 Olympics, she shattered the world record for the 100-meter and the 200-meter dashes, and became known as the world's fastest woman. She retired from track in 1989.

Nancy Marie Lopez (born 1957), from Torrance, California, began golfing with her father when she was eight. In 1978 Lopez won five Ladies Professional Golf Association (LPGA) tournaments in a row. After winning 35 tour tournaments, she qualified for the LPGA Hall of Fame in 1987.

FLORENCE GRIFFITH JOYNER ▶

▲ NANCY MARIE LOPEZ

WRITERS

◀ JACK LONDON

▼ JOHN STEINBECK

Jack London (1876–1916), one of the most popular writers of the early 1900s, was born in San Francisco. An adventurer who loved to travel, London followed the gold rush to Canada's Yukon Territory. His most famous book, *The Call of the Wild*, has been translated into more than 50 languages.

John Steinbeck (1902–1968) wrote prize-winning stories about the struggles of poor people. His best-known book, *The Grapes of Wrath*, tells the story of migrant workers who move from Oklahoma to California during the Great Depression. Much of Steinbeck's writing is set near his birthplace of Salinas, California.

Yoshiko Uchida (born 1921), from Alameda, California, writes stories for children about growing up Japanese American. Her books include *Journey to Topaz*, *The Sea of Gold and Other Tales from Japan*, *Samurai of Gold Hill*, and *Two Foolish Cats*.

Facts-at-a-Glance

Nickname: Golden State
Song: "I Love You, California"
Motto: *Eureka* ("I've found it")
Flower: golden poppy
Tree: California redwood
Bird: California valley quail
Animal: grizzly bear (now extinct in California)

Population: 29,839,250*
Rank in population, nationwide: 1st
Area: 163,707 sq miles (424,001 sq km)
Rank in area, nationwide: 3rd
Date and ranking of statehood:
   September 9, 1850, the 31st state
Capital: Sacramento
Major cities (and populations*):
   Los Angeles (3,485,398), San Diego (1,110,549),
   San Jose (782,248), San Francisco (723,959),
   Long Beach (429,433), Sacramento (369,365)
U.S. senators: 2
U.S. representatives: 52
Electoral votes: 54

Places to visit: Disneyland in Anaheim, Knott's
Berry Farm in Buena Park, Marine World Africa USA
in Vallejo, Yosemite National Park, Redwood
Highway in northern California, Universal Studios
in Los Angeles

Annual events: Tournament of Roses in Pasadena
(Jan.), Cherry Blossom Festival in San Francisco
(April), Teddy Bear Picnic in Crescent City (June),
Fort Bidwell Culture Exchange Pow Wow in Fort
Bidwell (July), Black Cowboy Parade in Oakland
(Oct.), International Festival of Masks in Los Angeles
(Oct.)

*1990 census

66

Natural resources: forests, oil, natural gas, sand and gravel, diatomite, gypsum, potash, pumice, tungsten, boron, gold

Agricultural products: milk, beef cattle, eggs, grapes, oranges, strawberries, apricots, olives, almonds, walnuts, avocados, lemons, melons, peaches, pears, plums, tomatoes, lettuce, cotton, hay

Manufactured goods: aircraft, spacecraft, cars, computers, canned fruits and vegetables, wines, soft drinks, videotape, telephone equipment, hardware

ENDANGERED SPECIES
Mammals—giant kangaroo rat, wolverine, blue whale, humpback whale, California bighorn sheep
Birds—bald eagle, peregrine falcon, light-footed clapper rail, California least tern, elf owl
Reptiles—loggerhead sea turtle, blunt-nosed leopard lizard, southern rubber boa
Fish—bull trout, bonytail, razorback sucker, desert pupfish, thicktail chub, unarmored threespine
Plants—marsh sandwort, slender-horned spineflower, seaside bird's-beak, San Diego button celery, San Francisco popcornflower

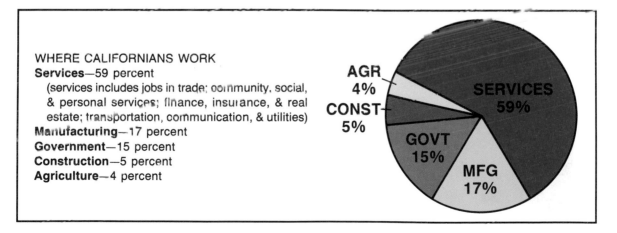

WHERE CALIFORNIANS WORK
Services—59 percent
(services includes jobs in trade; community, social, & personal services; finance, insurance, & real estate; transportation, communication, & utilities)
Manufacturing—17 percent
Government—15 percent
Construction—5 percent
Agriculture—4 percent

AGR
4%
CONST
5%
SERVICES
59%
GOVT
15%
MFG
17%

PRONUNCIATION GUIDE

Cabrillo, Juan Rodríguez
(kah-BREE-yoh, hwahn
rohth-REE-gayth)

Chumash (CHOO-mash)

Cinco de Mayo (SINK-oh duh MY-oh)

Monterey (mahnt-uh-RAY)

San Diego (san dee-AY-goh)

San Francisco (san fran-SIHS-koh)

San Joaquin (san wah-KEEN)

San Jose (san ho-ZAY)

Santa Cruz (sant-uh KROOZ)

Serra, Junípero
(SEHR-rah, hoo-NEE-peh-roh)

Sierra Nevada
(see-AYR-uh nuh-VAD-uh)

Yosemite (yoh-SEHM-uht-ee)

Glossary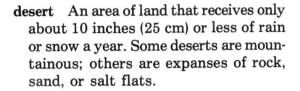

desert   An area of land that receives only about 10 inches (25 cm) or less of rain or snow a year. Some deserts are mountainous; others are expanses of rock, sand, or salt flats.

fault line   A break in the earth's crust where one side has moved up or down so that it no longer matches the other side. Earthquakes occur along fault lines.

fossil fuel   A material such as coal or oil that is formed in the earth from the remains of ancient plants and animals. Fossil fuels are used to produce power.

glacier   A large body of ice and snow that moves slowly over land.

immigrant   A person who moves into a foreign country and settles there.

68

irrigation A method of watering land by directing water through canals, ditches, pipes, or sprinklers.

Latino A person living in the United States who either came from or has ancestors from Latin America. Latin America includes Mexico and most of Central and South America.

mission A place where missionaries work. Missionaries are people sent out by a religious group to spread its beliefs to other peoples.

peninsula A stretch of land almost completely surrounded by water.

reservation Public land set aside by the government to be used by Native Americans.

smog A heavy haze that forms in the air when smoke and fog combine.

strait A narrow stretch of water that connects two larger bodies of water.

treaty An agreement between two or more groups, usually having to do with peace or trade.

69

Index ▰▰▰▰▰▰

Acknowledgments:

Maryland Cartographics, pp. 2, 11; Saul Mayer, pp. 2–3, 12 (left), 26; Nancy Hoyt Belcher, pp. 6, 13, 44 (left and right), 47 (left), 49 (lower left and right), 51; Jack Lindstrom, p. 7; © Shmuel Thaler, pp. 8, 19 (bottom), 44 (center), 46, 48, 49 (upper left), 54 (left), 60–61, 61 (bottom), 69; Laatsch-Hupp Photo: Henry J. Hupp, pp. 9, 45, David E. Trask, p. 17, C. W. Biedel, M.D., p. 59; Bonnie J. Fisher, p. 9 (inset); Diane Cooper, pp. 10, 56; Frederica Georgia, pp. 12 (right), 50 (right); Root Resources: © Kenneth W. Fink, p. 14, © Louise K. Broman, p. 18, © Alan G. Nelson, p. 19 (upper left), © Anthony Mercieca, p. 19 (right), © James Blank, pp. 42, 43, 52, 54–55, 58; Library of Congress, pp. 16–17, 37, 62 (upper left), 65 (lower left); Santa Barbara Museum of Natural History, p. 20; Bancroft Library, pp. 22 (left & right), 25, 27, 34; Print Coll., NY Public Library, p. 24; CA State Railroad Museum, p. 33; CA State Archives, p. 35; Coll. of the Santa Barbara Historical Museums, p. 36; League of Women Voters of LA Coll., CSU–Northridge, Urban Archives Center, photo by LA Fire Department, pp. 38–39; IPS, p. 41; Palm Springs Tourism, p. 47 (right); Betty Groskin, p. 50 (left); Doyen Salsig, p. 53; Special Collections, CA Polytechnic State University, p. 62 (upper right); Apple Computer, Inc., p. 62 (lower left & right); Hollywood Book and Poster, p. 63 (upper left, right, & center, lower left & center); Concert Express, p. 63 (lower right); City of LA, p. 64 (upper left); Sen. S. I. Hayakawa, p. 64 (upper right); The White House, p. 64 (center); New York Yankees, p. 64 (lower left); Mitchell B. Reibel / Sportschrome East / West, p. 65 (upper left); LPGA / Dee Darden, p. 65 (upper right); National Archives, Neg. No. 306–PS–C.59–11258, p. 65 (lower right); Dan Lerner, p. 71.